PET
DICTIONARY

An A to Z of animal companions

Author Don Harper
Editorial Manager Ruth Hooper
Editor Emily Hawkins
Art Director Miranda Kennedy
Art Editor Julia Harris
Production Director Clive Sparling
Consultant Zoologist Valerie Davies
Illustrators Sandra Doyle (The Art Agency), Wayne Ford (The Art Agency), Stuart Jackson-Carter (The Art Agency), Peter Scott (The Art Agency), Mark Stewart (The Art Agency), Gill Tomblin

Created and produced by
Andromeda Children's Books
An imprint of Pinwheel Ltd
Winchester House
259-269 Old Marylebone Road
London
NW1 5XJ
UK
www.pinwheel.co.uk

This edition produced in 2005 for Scholastic Inc.
Published by Tangerine Press, an imprint of Scholastic Inc.
557 Broadway, New York, NY 10012

Scholastic and Tangerine Press and associated logos are trademarks of Scholastic Inc.

ISBN 0-439-75459-3

Printed in China

Information Icons

Throughout this dictionary you will see icons next to each entry. These will give you more information about each creature listed.

Stars

These stars show you how easy or difficult each pet is to look after.

 Easy to care for

 Requires more attention

Suits an advanced caregiver

Habitat Icons

These icons show you the habitat each pet needs.

Aquarium

Cage, hutch, or aviary

Home roaming

Outdoor pond

Outdoors

Vivarium

Size Comparison Pictures

Next to each entry you will see a symbol, either a hand or a man, next to a red icon of each animal listed. The symbol shows you the size of each animal in real life.

7 inches

The first symbol is a human adult's hand, which measures about 7 inches (18 cm) from the wrist to the tip of the longest finger. Some animals are smaller than this, so this comparison shows you its size.

6 feet

The second symbol is an adult human. With its arms outstretched, the armspan measures about 6 feet (1.8 m). This symbol shows the size of really big animals.

The size of each dog and cat in this book is given as the height from the floor to the top of the shoulder.

PET
DICTIONARY

An A to Z of animal companions

tangerine Press®

an imprint of

■SCHOLASTIC

www.scholastic.com

The world of pets

Tarantula

Pets are animals that are kept by people as companions. There are many different types of pets, from all of the main animal groups. Some pets need to be kept inside and require special housing, while others can live outdoors.

Invertebrates

Invertebrates are animals without a backbone or internal skeleton. They include insects like walking sticks, which have six legs, and spiders such as tarantulas, which have eight legs. Most invertebrates are small and fragile, but some can defend themselves by giving a nasty bite.

Fish

All fish live underwater and breathe through gills on the sides of their heads. They can take oxygen directly from the water, so they do not have to come up to the surface to breathe. Most fish lay eggs, and sometimes, one or both of the parents look after the eggs and care for the young after they have hatched.

Neon tetra

Amphibians

Frogs, toads, newts, and salamanders are all types of amphibians. They live in damp areas and come back to the water to breed. Most amphibians lay jelly-covered eggs in water, which hatch into tadpoles. The tadpoles develop into adult amphibians and may live on land.

White's tree frog

Reptiles

Reptiles are called "cold-blooded" because their bodies do not produce heat. They rely on their environment for warmth, so they live mainly in hot countries. Reptiles include snakes, lizards, tortoises, and turtles. Some give birth to live young, but many lay eggs. Reptiles eat a wide range of foods—snakes hunt other animals, but tortoises feed mainly on plants.

Green iguana

Birds

All birds have a body covering of feathers, which keeps them warm and allows them to fly. A female bird, called a hen, lays hard-shelled eggs, from which the young, known as chicks, will hatch. Members of the parrot family are popular as pets because they can mimic words. They often have brightly-colored feathers.

Zebra finch

Old English sheepdog

Mammals

Dogs and cats are both members of this group, as are rats and rabbits. All mammals have hair, and the females suckle their young with milk. Some pet mammals, such as dogs, are very different from their wild relatives, both in the way they look and their behavior. They are divided into breeds.

Choosing and keeping a pet

Deciding what type of pet you would like is always exciting, but there are many factors you need to consider. Some pets are harder to look after than others and need more time spent on them. Certain pets can also be expensive to buy and house.

Indian walking stick

Invertebrates

These pets are not likely to become friendly, but they are interesting to watch. Most invertebrates are not difficult to house or expensive to look after, so they are a good choice if you are saving up your pocket money. Invertebrates often live for up to a year, but tarantulas can have a much longer lifespan.

Fish

Many fish need to be kept in warm water, but goldfish can be kept in an aquarium without a heater. Fish that require salt water are the most difficult to keep. Some fish, such as koi, will grow too large for a home aquarium.

Paradise fish

Amphibians

Shy by nature, amphibians are often brightly colored. This serves as a warning to other animals that their skin contains poison—so you need to handle them very carefully. You can also injure their skin easily if you pick them up with dry hands.

Japanese fire-bellied newt

Reptiles

A pet reptile should be housed in a heated enclosure called a vivarium. This must have special lighting to keep the reptile healthy. On warm days, it may be possible to allow a tortoise out into a run in the garden. Many tortoises sleep, or hibernate, through the winter.

Painted turtle

Birds

In the case of the parrot family, only young birds will become really tame and learn to talk well. Most pet birds eat seeds and also need grit. This contains tiny stones that help grind up the seeds in a bird's stomach. Birds cannot chew their food like us, because they have no teeth.

Parrotlet

Rex rabbit

Mammals

For people living in cities, small mammals such as rabbits and rodents make good pets because they can live safely in the home in hutches or cages. Larger mammals such as cats and dogs need more exercise, so they suit owners with plenty of outdoor space.

Aa

Abyssinian cat

Average height: 9 inches (23 cm)

The Abyssinian cat is one of the oldest known breeds of cats. In fact, many believe it is a relative of the African wildcat, ancestor of all domestic cats. Although not considered a "lap cat," it is energetic, curious, and loyal. Unlike most cats, many Abyssinians love to play in water. The Abyssinian is a short-haired, long-legged, graceful cat.

American shorthair cat

Average height: 9 inches (23 cm)

American shorthairs look somewhat like ordinary alley cats, but they are larger and have rounder faces. They have been bred in many different colors and coat patterns. The American shorthair is a very popular pet in North America because it is affectionate and playful. It is often seen at shows—its short coat needs little grooming to look good.

Max length: 3½ inches (8 cm)

Anemone fish ★★★

The anemone fish lives among sea anemones on coral reefs. It is a brightly colored fish that swims slowly, so it is an easy target for predators. But, if threatened, it can dart out of sight among the stinging tentacles of the anemone. These tentacles do not hurt the fish, but they give it somewhere safe to hide.

Anemone fish are often called clownfish because of their colorful, clownlike patterning.

Fact
There is only one male and one female in a group of anemone fish. If the female dies, the male becomes a new female and one of the young becomes the new male.

Max length: 6 inches (15 cm)

Angelfish ★★

This tropical fish needs a tall aquarium because of its height. Its narrow body means it can swim very easily among reeds to escape from danger. In the wild, the female angelfish lays her eggs on a leaf or a rock. In an aquarium, she will often lay them on a piece of slate. Both parents guard the eggs and watch over the young after they hatch.

Aa

Angora rabbit ★★★

Max length: 16 inches (41 cm)

The soft wool of the angora rabbit is very valuable. It is often used to make warm clothing. When this rabbit molts, or sheds, its wool is collected by hand grooming. It needs plenty of grooming to prevent its coat from becoming matted. Angora rabbits are normally kept indoors in wire pens to keep their coats clean. White angoras are common, but other colors have also been bred.

Max length: 8 inches (20 cm)

Axolotl ★

Fact
If an axolotl's limb is accidentally bitten off in a feeding frenzy, it can grow a new one.

The axolotl (pronounced ax-o-lot-ul) is the big kid of the amphibian world—it might spend its whole life as a giant tadpole, never becoming an adult. However, if the water level in its aquarium falls, or there is iodine in the water, then it will change into a salamander. It starts to breathe air and the gills on the sides of its head shrink back. Axolotls feed on small worms and similar creatures.

Bearded dragon ⭐⭐

Max length: 20 inches (50 cm)

The bearded dragon may look fierce, but in the wild it is largely vegetarian. As a pet, it eats plants and some insects. It must be kept in a vivarium: a warm enclosure with a special light. Young bearded dragons can become very tame. This lizard, which can live for up to 10 years, communicates by bobbing its head.

Bengal cat ⭐

Average height: 10 inches (25 cm)

Some domestic cats, such as the Bengal, have markings that look like those of wild cats. The Bengal was bred by mating a wild Asian leopard cat with a domestic cat. The resulting kittens were born with the wild cat's spotted patterning. The Bengal is one of the most highly-prized and expensive cats. Those with very pale coats are called snow leopards.

Betta ⭐⭐

Max length: 2¾ inches (7 cm)

The male betta is one of the most colorful fish, but his beauty hides a deadly secret. Two males must never be kept in the same aquarium, because they will fight to the death. Do not place a mirror next to the aquarium, because a male betta will attack his own reflection.

Birman cat

Average height: 9 inches (23 cm)

The Birman is a breed of mystery. Today's Birmans are related to a cat that was given as a gift to two European explorers more than 80 years ago. These explorers traveled through the Asian country of Burma (now called Myanmar). On their journey, they helped some monks fight off an attack on the temple where these cats were kept. Nobody is sure whether Birmans still exist in their homeland today.

Fact
The white areas on the front paws of the Birman are called gloves, while those on its hind paws are known as socks.

Bombay cat

Average height: 9 inches (23 cm)

The short, shiny, black coat of the Bombay looks like that of a black panther, which is a type of leopard. The Bombay also has attractive copper-colored eyes.

It was bred by mating American shorthairs with Burmese cats in the U.S. Now, similar cats are also being bred in Europe. The breed is named after a major Indian city.

British shorthair cat ⭐

Average height: 10 inches (25 cm)

Large and cuddly, British shorthairs are affectionate and friendly by nature. They are bred in many colors, including brown, orange, and blue. Although short, the breed's fur is thick, giving protection and warmth in cold weather. These cats are usually active and can adapt to a variety of living conditions, including households with children and other pets.

Budgerigar ⭐

Max length: 7 inches (18 cm)

With the ability to learn up to 800 words, this talkative bird is considered the most popular cage bird in the world. Domestic budgerigars are bred in a wide range of colors, including gray, blue, violet, yellow, and white. Budgerigars are easy to care for, have lots of personality, and love companionship.

Burmese cat ⭐

Average height: 9 inches (23 cm)

The traditional color associated with the Burmese breed is brown, but these cats are bred in many other colors, including pale cream and tangerine-red. The cat's coat is very sleek because its hair lies flat against its body, showing off its athletic shape. The Burmese likes plenty of attention and is very affectionate in return.

Cc

Average height: 9 inches
(23 cm)

California spangled cat ⭐

This rare breed was the idea of a Hollywood scriptwriter who wanted to create a long-legged domestic cat that looked like a miniature cheetah. After many years of mixing breeds, the program worked. Although the California spangled cat may look like a tiny wild cheetah, it makes an affectionate, social, and devoted house pet.

Max length: 5¾ inches (14.5 cm)

Canary ⭐

The cock canary's beautiful song makes it a popular pet. Although their ancestors were green, canaries today come in many different colors. This bird is easy to care for, and because it is not particularly social, it does not need much attention. Cock birds can quarrel with each other, so they are kept on their own as pets.

Chihuahua ★

Max height: 12 inches (30 cm)

The tiny Chihuahua is the smallest dog in the world. It is named after the Mexican state of Chihuahua. A Chihuahua must be handled carefully, because it has a hole under its skin in the center of its skull. This means that its brain is not fully protected by bone. In spite of its size, this dog can bark surprisingly loudly.

Fact
Chihuahuas may shiver frequently, even if they are wearing a coat. This is often a sign of excitement, not of being cold.

Chinchilla ★★

Max length: 15 inches (38 cm)

The chinchilla comes from the Andes mountains of South America, where its soft, thick fur protects it from the cold. Gnawing on wooden branches helps prevent this rodent's teeth from becoming overgrown. The chinchilla also needs a special dust bath to keep its fur in good condition. It is nocturnal, so it is most active during the night.

Cc

Chipmunk ★★

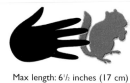

Max length: 6½ inches (17 cm)

A chipmunk looks a bit like a squirrel, complete with a bushy tail. They are both rodents and have many similar characteristics. Like squirrels, chipmunks are very active and agile, climbing and jumping from branch to branch. As a pet, a chipmunk needs to be kept in a strong, aviary-type enclosure, with plenty of branches to run along and a snug nest box to sleep in.

Max length: 12½ inches (32 cm)

Cockatiel ★

The cockatiel's most obvious feature is its crest. It will raise these long, narrow feathers when it is excited or frightened. Like other parrots, a pet cockatiel can be taught to talk and can also learn to whistle tunes quite easily. The natural call of the cockatiel is much quieter than those of most parrots.

Fact
Lutino cockatiels are now very popular. They were originally called moonbeams, after their breeder—a Mrs. Moon.

Corn snake ★★

Max length: 6 feet (1.8 m)

This snake got its name because the patterns on its belly resemble Indian corn kernels. Selective breeding of corn snakes in captivity has produced many colorful variations. Corn snakes eat mice, and as they grow, they shed their skins regularly. They are known for their ability to escape, so their living quarters need to be tightly fitted with a vented cover.

Corydoras catfish ★★

Max length: 6 inches (15 cm)

Corydoras catfish means "little armored catfish." Also known as "cory cats," these fish prefer to live near the bottom of the aquarium. They have spiky projections, called barbels, around their mouths. These help them find worms and other food. They are especially useful when the water is muddy, making it difficult to see.

Dd

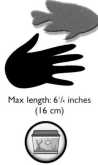

Max length: 6¼ inches (16 cm)

Damselfish ★★★

Damselfish vary in color. They are often a brilliant blue or different shades of blue and green. They can be kept easily in saltwater aquariums. However, damselfish can be aggressive with others, so they should not be kept together. In the wild, they live in tropical seas all over the world.

Fact
The male damselfish swims around his mate in circles and makes strange chirping calls to drive off rival males.

Max length: 12 inches (30 cm)

Degu ★★

These rodents were originally kept to investigate the illness diabetes, which they can suffer if they have an unsuitable diet. Today, however, they have become popular as pets. They need special food pellets (as sold for chinchillas) to keep them healthy. They can also eat hay. Because degus are social animals, it is important for them to interact with other degus.

Average height: 9 inches (23 cm)

Devon rex

These cats are often compared to "pixies" because of their big ears, angular faces, and mischievous personalities. Devon rexes are curious, people-loving cats. They communicate with chirps and chortles rather than the typical "meow." They have even been known to wag their tails and play fetch like dogs.

Discus ★★

Max length: 7 inches (18 cm)

These beautiful aquarium fish are much brighter in color than their wild relatives. Discus fish guard their eggs and feed their young when the eggs hatch. Both parents produce a "milk" on their bodies that the young nibble. The discus' slim, round body is a similar shape to the discus thrown in athletics.

Dutch rabbit ★

Max length: 18 inches (45 cm)

Attractive and friendly, Dutch rabbits are popular pets. Because they are easy-going and small, they adapt well to indoor cages. Caring for a Dutch rabbit involves grooming, cleaning its cage often, and refilling its food and water supply. They eat vegetables and special pellets sold at pet supply stores.

Ee

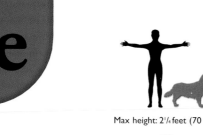

Max height: 2¼ feet (70 cm)

Eskimo dog ★★

The Eskimo dog has always been a very important companion for native people living in the Arctic region. These dogs are still used today to pull sleds in teams and to help on hunting trips. They are very strong and well-protected against the cold by their thick coats. The Eskimo dog has a wolflike face and a tail that curls over its back.

Average height: 10 inches (25 cm)

Exotic cat ★

One of the most popular breeds in the U.S., the exotic cat makes a quiet, sweet, loyal companion. A cross between a Persian and an American shorthair cat, it has the endearing characteristics of a Persian without the high maintenance of its long coat. Exotic cats come in many colors and all share a cuddly appearance.

Ferret ★★

Max length: 14 inches (36 cm)

Cousins of weasels, skunks, and otters, ferrets are lively and entertaining domestic animals. Ferrets require a lot of care, as much care as a dog or a cat, and they have a distinct musklike smell that some find unpleasant. The ferret life span is between six and ten years.

Fact
A pet ferret can be taught to do tricks like a dog and to use a litter box like a cat.

Finnish spitz ★★

Max height: 20 inches (50 cm)

The Finnish spitz is a breed of dog that has upright, pointed ears and reddish fur. It was first kept as a hunting companion, barking to alert its owner when it spotted a target. In competitions today, these dogs are judged on the number of times they can bark in a minute. Some can bark as often as 160 times a minute.

Ff

Max length: 11 inches (28 cm)

Fire salamander ★

The stunning color of this amphibian helps explain its name. Most fire salamanders have yellow and black markings, although some are orange and black. They are shy by nature and like damp surroundings, so they often hide under rocks and in moss. Fire salamanders are nocturnal, they hibernate during the winter, and they can live to be more than 20 years old!

Max length: 9¾ inches (25 cm)

Four-eyed fish ★★★

In reality, the four-eyed fish has only two eyes. Each eye is divided into two sections, so it can see as if it had four eyes. It spends much of its time near the surface, and its eyes allow it to see above and below the water at the same time. Four-eyed fish can be kept alone or with others, and they are not picky eaters.

Garter snake ★★

Max length: 4¼ feet
(1.3 m)

The agile garter snake has a very slender body shape. It often lives in damp areas, so it must have a bowl of water in its enclosure. This snake feeds on frogs, fish, and earthworms. Once tame, it can be picked up easily, but a nervous garter snake may squirt an unpleasant smelling substance from its rear end.

German shepherd ★

Max height: 2¼ feet
(65 cm)

Bred originally to watch over sheep, the German shepherd dog is known for its bravery. It acted as a messenger dog in wartime, and it is used by many police forces today. This breed has been trained to find people missing in snowstorms or trapped in earthquake-stricken buildings. German shepherd dogs are also kept as guide dogs for the blind.

Goat ★★

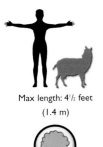

Max length: 4½ feet
(1.4 m)

Goats live outside, so they need an area of grass and a shelter. A young goat, called a kid, can be tamed quite easily and trained to walk on a leash. Female goats are popular as pets, because they do not have the same strong smell as the male, known as the billy.

Gg

Max height: 1¹¹/₁₂ feet (58 cm)

Golden retriever ★

The golden retriever is one of the most popular dog breeds in the world. This retriever is an excellent swimmer and was originally bred to find ducks that had been shot down over water. The dog's strong tail acts like a ship's rudder, helping it steer through the water. In spite of their name, some golden retrievers have much lighter coats than others.

Max length: 10 inches (25 cm)

Goldfish ★

The most common household pet in the world, the goldfish has a lifespan of five to ten years and can provide its owner with a lot of enjoyment. Available in most pet stores, the goldfish is easy to care for and inexpensive. Goldfish are dark colored when they are young, but a brighter orange when they grow older.

Gray parrot ⭐

Max length: 13 inches (33 cm)

The gray parrot is considered to be the most talented talking bird in the world. Some can say more than 700 different words. They learn very fast while they are young. A gray parrot can even understand the meanings of some words, so it can ask for its favorite food or toy. They can live for up to 70 years.

Green iguana ⭐⭐⭐

Max length: 6 feet (1.8 m)

A green iguana is less than a foot long when it hatches from its egg; but in just a few years it will grow to between four and six feet long. Although green iguanas can eat both plants and meat, they usually eat plants. They communicate using a variety of different body gestures. Caring for a pet iguana requires a lot of work and space, and can be expensive.

Max height: 2½ feet (76 cm)

Greyhound ⭐

The naturally gentle greyhound is the champion sprinter of the dog world. Its strong back legs help it run very fast over short distances. The greyhound is an ancient breed that was used for hunting thousands of years ago by the Greeks and Romans. Today, greyhound racing is popular in many countries.

Hh

Max length: 1³/₄ inches (4.5 cm)

Hatchetfish

A hatchet is a tool with a sharp blade, a bit like an ax. This fish is so-called because its body is shaped like a small hatchet. It has a broad, flat top to its body, which narrows to a bladelike underside. Living close to the water's surface, a hatchetfish may sometimes leap out of the water to catch flying insects.

Max height: 13³/₄ inches (35 cm)

Fact
The Havanese is thought to be a relative of the Bichon breeds from southern Europe. It is also called the Bichon Havanais.

Havanese dog

The Havanese is a small dog with a long coat that hangs down the sides of its face. Its name comes from Havana, the capital of Cuba. It is believed that the ancestors of the Havanese dog were brought to Cuba from the Canary Islands by sailors many years ago.

Hermit crab ★★

Max length: 4 inches (10 cm)

The hermit crab is easy to care for and entertaining. It lives inside a shell that it carries around to protect itself. As it grows larger, a pet hermit crab needs to be given a new home before it outgrows its old shell. Bigger shells can be found at pet supply stores, and they should be placed inside the crab's enclosure.

Average height: 10 inches (25 cm)

Himalayan cat ★★

The Himalayan cat is a large, short, heavy-bodied cat that is low to the ground. Considered part of the Persian cat family, the Himalayan was developed by mixing Persian cats with Siamese cats. Well-known for their blue eyes and long, soft coats, they are said to be friendly, affectionate, and mischievous.

Ii

Max height: 2¹/₃ feet (70 cm)

Ibizan hound ⭐

Dogs that look like Ibizan hounds have been found in ancient Egyptian pictures that are over 5,000 years old. This suggests that the breed has been kept in the Mediterranean region for a very long time. The Ibizan hound has excellent eyesight and very large ears, which help it hear well. It also has an athletic body, and requires a lot of regular exercise.

Max length: 11¹/₂ inches (29 cm)

Indian walking stick ⭐

This insect looks like the plants on which it feeds, so it is hard to spot. If touched, a walking stick will let go of its branch and fall to the ground like an old twig. The Indian walking stick is simple to raise and eats plants, including bramble leaves and lettuce. Its cage must be kept very clean because eventually it will contain many eggs.

Japanese bobtail cat ★

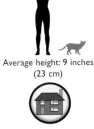

Average height: 9 inches
(23 cm)

This unusual breed has a short, twisted tail. In Japan, these cats were first kept as a way of stopping mice from eating rice paper, which was used as writing paper. The breed was also believed to bring good luck. The Japanese bobtail is strong-willed, active, and energetic, but very affectionate to its family. It demands lots of attention, because it gets bored easily.

Fact
The mi-ke (pronounced mee-kay) is the most popular variety of Japanese bobtail. Its coat is made up of red, black, and white areas.

Japanese fire-bellied newt ★

Max length: 4¾ inches (12 cm)

This pet is relatively easy to care for; however, careful preparations need to be made for its proper housing. This amphibian is dark brown with a bright reddish-orange underbelly. It has poisons in its skin and, in the wild, its bright color serves as a warning to predators. Pet newts are hardy eaters when fed different kinds of worms and shrimp.

Jj

Max length: 4 inches (10 cm)

Jewel cichlid ★★

This fish is a good pet because it is easy to care for. However, it is an aggressive fish, so a pair is best kept away from others in a well-planted aquarium. These fish often appear dull in color at the pet store, but in the mating season, they display some stunning colors. As parents, jewel cichlids guard their young with fierce determination.

Max length: 6 inches (15 cm)

Fact
Jirds are able to sit up on their hindquarters so they can look around. In the wild, this helps them spot danger more easily.

Jird ★★

Although bigger in size, jirds are members of the same family as the common gerbil. They are lively, entertaining, low-maintenance pets. Jirds love to burrow in their cages and can be fed vegetables, fruit, seeds, and store-bought pellets. They are clean, odorless animals, which makes them popular rodents to keep.

Max height: 18 inches (45 cm)

Keeshond ⭐

A typical housedog and companion, the keeshond makes a great watchdog because of its clear bark and excellent hearing. Affectionate and loving toward its family, this dog gets along well with children and other pets. It requires lots of regular grooming.

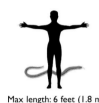

Max length: 6 feet (1.8 m)

Kingsnake ⭐⭐

Kingsnakes make good reptilian pets because they are easy to tame and handle. The most important factor in keeping a pet kingsnake is providing the correct environmental conditions. In captivity, most are fed mice; but in the wild, the kingsnake's diet also includes other snakes.

Max length: 11¾ inches (30 cm)

Kissing gourami ⭐⭐

These fish will often lock their lips together so it looks as if they are kissing. This is actually a display of aggression. This "kissing" is mostly used to scrape algae off of rocks. The kissing gourami eats a wide range of foods, including small live foods. Its tank must be kept clean and at a constant water temperature.

Kk

Koi

Max length: 3 feet (90 cm)

Koi is a Japanese word meaning "golden carp." Its large size means that it needs to be kept in ponds. At shows, a koi's body shape, color, and markings are important to the judges. Some koi are so valuable that they can sell for the cost of a home. They are very long-lived fish, with a possible lifespan of over 80 years.

Korat cat

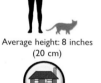

Average height: 8 inches (20 cm)

So-called "blue" cats, such as the Korat, are actually gray in color. This breed also has a silver tinge to its coat and deep green eyes. The Korat is named after an area in Thailand. Known for its sweet but independent character, the Korat bonds well with its owners and gets along with children.

Fact
The Korat is known in Thailand as the Si Sawat, because its coat is the same color as the nuts from the Sawat tree.

Max length: 10 inches (25 cm)

Leopard gecko ⭐

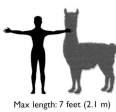

This lizard comes from a hot, dry part of the world. An adult leopard gecko has a spotted pattern similar to the wild cat it is named after. Relatively clean animals, leopard geckos are among the easiest lizards to maintain. These nocturnal animals rarely bite and can be easily tamed. A leopard gecko should be fed insects, available at most pet supply stores.

Max length: 7 feet (2.1 m)

Llama ⭐⭐⭐

Entertaining and easy to train, pet llamas are used to cold, dry weather because they come from the high Andes mountains in South America. Llamas are intelligent, gentle, clean animals that live for 15 to 20 years. They come in a variety of colors, sizes, and wool types, and owners even report that they have different personalities.

Ll

Max length: 18 inches (45 cm)

Lop, dwarf rabbit

There are several types of lop rabbits. As they grow, their ears fold and hang down over the sides of the head, setting them apart from other rabbits, which have ears that stand up straight. A rabbit is an intelligent animal and can be trained to use a litter box. This allows it to be let out of its cage for periods of supervised play in the house.

Max length: 5¾ inches (14.5 cm)

Lovebird

Lovebirds are small parrots with short, square tails. They are called lovebirds because the cock and hen like to stay close to each other. A pair of lovebirds will groom each other's feathers with their bills. This behavior is known as preening. A young lovebird can be taught to whistle and even to say a few words. It can also become very tame, perching on its owner's fingers.

Maine coon cat ★★

Average height: 10 inches (25 cm)

The Maine coon is the largest domestic cat in the world. It comes from Maine, where its ancestors were brought from Europe, and it is one of the oldest natural breeds of North America. Maine coons often have ringed tabby markings on their tails, like those seen on raccoons—this explains the unusual second part of their name. Their coats grow long and thick during the winter, when the weather is cold.

Fact
Manx cats are a symbol of the Isle of Man. They have appeared on the island's coins and postage stamps.

Manx cat ★

Average height: 9 inches (23 cm)

Although they are often known as the tailless breed, some Manx cats do have a tail, or a "stump," which can vary in length. The Manx are affectionate cats that get along well with children and dogs. They make ideal family pets and adapt well to indoor life. A Manx cat's lifespan is between 10 and 12 years.

Mm

Molly ★★

Max length: 7 inches (18 cm)

Although most molly fish are black or speckled, there are 21 different color variations in total. Mollies need an aquarium that is not overcrowded, but well planted to attract algae. They are peaceful fish that are not too demanding, and make great pets. Female mollies are larger than males, and they can produce as many as 300 babies at a time.

Fact
A Mongolian gerbil must be handled gently, otherwise it may play dead—a tactic it uses in the wild.

Mongolian gerbil ★

Max length: 5 inches (13 cm)

The strong back legs of the Mongolian gerbil allow it to hop and jump well. These rodents live together in groups. A Mongolian gerbil must never be caught by the tip of its tail. If this happens, the delicate tip will break off, allowing the gerbil to scamper away—just as if it was being chased by a predator.

Mouse

Max length: 4 inches (11 cm)

A female mouse, called a doe, makes a better pet than a male (or buck) because she produces less odor. Mice have been bred in many colors, so you can choose from colors including white, red, black, and even multicolored! Never give your mouse a playwheel with an open tread, because its tail may become trapped as the wheel spins.

Fact

A young mynah bird is called a gaper, because of the way it opens its bill wide, hoping to be fed.

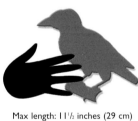

Mynah bird

Max length: 11½ inches (29 cm)

This popular member of the starling family can be taught to talk and whistle tunes quite easily. A mynah bird may even learn other noises, such as the ringing of a telephone, so well that it is difficult to tell this sound apart from the real thing! Mynahs feed mainly on fruits and insects, and love to bathe in a pot of water.

Nn

Max length: 1½ inches (4 cm)

Neon tetra ★★

The bright stripes running down each side of this fish's body are similar in color to the green and red neon lights seen along busy city streets at night. These beautiful fish were once so rare that they were extremely expensive when they first became available. Today, they are bred in large numbers and are much cheaper to buy.

Fact
Female neon tetras will often lay 200 tiny eggs at a time. These hatch very quickly, in just a day or two.

Max length: 12 inches (30 cm)

Netherland dwarf rabbit ★

This little rabbit has short ears and a round head. Its fur is short and soft, and can be many different colors. In spite of its appealing size, it is not always friendly, and is best suited to older children. The Netherland dwarf rabbit can live seven years or more.

Norwegian forest cat

★ ★

Average height: 10 inches (25 cm)

In Norway today, this semi-long-coated breed is often seen on farms. In the spring, it sheds its heavy coat down to a much lighter one. When its tail is fanned to its fullest, it can be as long as 12 inches (30 cm). A fairly large breed, the Norwegian forest cat has a life expectancy of 10 to 12 years, and is loyal and affectionate to its owner.

Nova Scotia duck tolling retriever

★ ★

Max height: 20½ inches (52 cm)

This dog got its unusual name because it was used to attract curious ducks during a hunt. It looks like a small golden retriever and is an excellent companion. Many owners report that their dogs have life-saving instincts. This playful pet is well-behaved, but needs a lot of exercise. The popularity of this dog continues to grow as more people learn about the breed.

Oo

Max height: 1⅚ feet (55 cm)

Old English sheepdog ★★

This lively dog was originally used to help farmers with sheep. It herded them to market and made sure that none were left behind along the way. The long coat of an old English sheepdog needs plenty of grooming to keep it from becoming matted, although sometimes its hair may be clipped back quite short. This large breed needs plenty of exercise to stay in shape.

Max length: 4 inches (10 cm)

Orange chromide ⭐⭐

The orange chromide is a member of the large cichlid family of fish. It is unusual because it is one of only three types of cichlid found in Asia, and it often lives in salty rather than freshwater. Orange chromides are devoted parents. Both members of the pair guard their eggs and watch over the young when they hatch.

Max length: 2 feet (60 cm)

Orfe ⭐

The orfe is a pond fish that can grow to be quite large. It has a slim body shape and can swim fast. If an orfe stays close to the surface, especially near a fountain on a hot day, this is seen as a sign that a thunderstorm is approaching. They have been bred in various colors, but the golden orfe is the most popular.

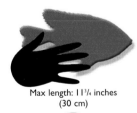

Max length: 11¾ inches (30 cm)

Oscar ⭐⭐

Each oscar fish has its own individual patterning. Some have a white rather than a dark background coloring. An oscar makes a great pet: it will soon learn to recognize its owner and can be taught to take food from the hand. This member of the cichlid family has a large mouth and an appetite to match. It can be somewhat aggressive, and could even eat other fish in its aquarium.

Oo

41

Pp

Painted turtle ★★

Max length: 10 inches (25 cm)

This reptile's bright markings explain why it is called a "painted" turtle. They are particularly noticeable on the underside of its shell. Although this turtle spends much of its time in the water, it comes out regularly to sunbathe on land. Painted turtles are omnivores: they eat fish, insects, aquatic plants, and fruits.

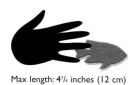

Max length: 4¾ inches (12 cm)

Paradise fish ★★

With bright colors and bold stripes, the male paradise fish can be very attractive. Male paradise fish must not be kept in the same water as other males, as they can become aggressive. Paradise fish enjoy eating flake food, ghost shrimp, and even baby fish. They are very active fish, darting and gliding through the water, so a large tank is recommended.

Parrotlet

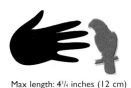

Max length: 4¾ inches (12 cm)

The parrotlet is becoming one of the most popular pet birds. It is small with beautifully colored feathers and an intelligent, curious nature. Capable of bonding with its owners and talking, this comical bird makes an excellent companion. This cousin of the Amazon parrot can live to be over 20 years old.

Fact

In an aviary, a hen parrotlet lays her white eggs in a nest box. In the wild, she uses a hollow tree. The eggs hatch after three weeks.

Persian cat

Average height: 10 inches (25 cm)

The Persian cat has a broad, flat face and short legs. Its long coat and bushy tail mean it has to be groomed every day to prevent its fur from becoming matted. Although the first Persian cats were white, they are now bred in a wide range of colors and patterns. They are friendly cats and usually stay close to home.

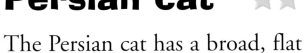

Pp

Max length: 3 inches (8 cm)

Platy ★★

Many platies are a fiery shade of orangey-red, and breeders often give them a special food that helps deepen this color. Platies are very popular because they can be kept with other platies or with different types of fish. They are also easy to breed. Females, which are larger than males, give birth to live young rather than laying eggs.

Fact
There are 20 different types of platy. The tuxedo platy's rear half is black, and the wagtail has black fins and lips.

Max length: 9 inches (23 cm)

Pygmy hedgehog ★

The pygmy hedgehog makes a cuddly pet in spite of its sharp spines. With a lifespan of six to eight years, this quirky creature can bring lots of enjoyment if it is given proper care. It is illegal to keep a pet hedgehog in some states in the U.S.

Max length: 5 inches (13 cm)

Quail, button

★★

The button quail is a small, neat, and relatively quiet bird. Nervous by nature, it can become quite tame with positive encouragement, such as rewarding it with meal worms. Owners report that button quail are sweet, amusing, active birds that make great pets.

Qq

Fact
Button quails' feet are designed for walking, not perching. Their living quarters should be prepared with this in mind.

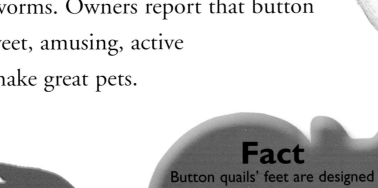

Max length: 12 inches (30 cm)

Quetzal cichlid

★★

The quetzal bird is a stunning creature with red feathers that lives in the Central American rain forest. This cichlid fish gets its name from the quetzal bird—it comes from the same area, and also has bright red coloring. As it grows older, the male develops a hump on its head, which sets it apart from the females. An adult pair of quetzal cichlids will need a large aquarium.

Rr

Average height: 10 inches (25 cm)

Ragdoll cat ★★

When a person carries a ragdoll cat, it usually relaxes, appearing limp and floppy just like the doll that it is named after. This cat is often called a "gentle giant," and it is for this reason that it is best kept as an indoor pet. It lacks an aggressive nature so it relies on protection from its owners. The ragdoll can live for up to 20 years.

Fact
The way in which a ragdoll cat relaxes when it is picked up and carried is described by breeders as its "flop factor."

Max length: 11 inches (28 cm)

Rat ★★

Rats make intelligent, friendly pets that can live up to four years. Although they are curious, social animals that are easily tamed, they are not easy pets to look after. They require cage cleaning, feeding, and regular exercise. Pet rats do best when kept with other rats of the same sex.

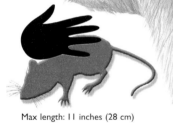

Rat snake ★★

Max length: 8 feet (2.4 m)

As its name suggests, the rat snake feeds on rats and other rodents. Some rat snakes can become tame if they are obtained young and handled regularly. Snakes must not be squeezed tightly, as this can cause serious injury. A rat snake should be kept in a vivarium with some strong branches for it to climb.

Rr

Max length: 16 inches (40 cm)

Rex rabbit ★

The rex rabbit has the softest, shortest fur of all rabbits. This means that it can become cold living outdoors in the winter, so its hutch may have to be brought inside. Many rexes are a chocolate brown color, but you can choose from other colors too, including lilac and white. The smallest type of rex rabbit is known as the mini rex.

Rr

Max length: 4 inches (10 cm)

Russian hamster ⭐

Smaller than its Syrian relation, the Russian hamster is also more friendly with others of its own kind. It may be possible for two Russian hamsters to live side by side without fighting if they are kept together from an early age. Some Russian hamsters have white coats during the winter. In the wild, this helps them hide on the snowy ground.

Average height: 9 inches (23 cm)

Russian shorthair cat ⭐

Quiet, sensitive, and sometimes shy, the Russian shorthair is a loyal and devoted cat. Once settled in a loving environment, this cat enjoys playing with toys, climbing, and jumping about. It appreciates human affection, but does not need a lot of grooming. Some owners report that their cats sometimes appear "hurt" when rejected.

Scottish fold cat ⭐

Average height: 9 inches (23 cm)

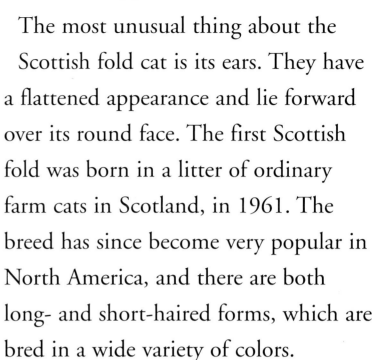

The most unusual thing about the Scottish fold cat is its ears. They have a flattened appearance and lie forward over its round face. The first Scottish fold was born in a litter of ordinary farm cats in Scotland, in 1961. The breed has since become very popular in North America, and there are both long- and short-haired forms, which are bred in a wide variety of colors.

Siamese cat ⭐

Average height: 8 inches (20 cm)

The sleek Siamese cat has a triangular head and a long, narrow body. Its face is darker in color than its body, as are its ears, paws, and tail. Siamese can be very noisy cats, and demand a lot of attention from their owners. They are also eager climbers, both around the home and in the backyard.

Ss

Society finch

Max length: 5 inches (13 cm)

The sociable nature of this popular finch explains its name. This friendly bird lives with other society finches in small groups. It makes a great pet because it does not become stressed as easily as other species. As a result, it can live happily with other birds and even other pets. It is very comfortable with humans and easy to tame.

Sphynx cat

Average height: 8 inches (20 cm)

In spite of being called the hairless cat, the Sphynx does have some hair, especially on its head, tail, and feet. Its body is covered with very short fur, which is like the fuzzy skin on a peach. The Sphynx prefers to live indoors, where it is warm. This also saves its delicate skin from becoming burned on sunny days.

Max length: 4 inches (10 cm)

Swordtail ★★

Only the male swordtail develops the long spike on the end of its tail. Most wild swordtails are green, but aquarium swordtails are bred in a much wider range of colors, such as deep orange. Only keep one male in an aquarium alongside females, otherwise weaker males will be bullied. Males can be kept together safely without females.

Fact
Some types of swordtail are named after the cities where they were first bred, such as the Wiesbaden variety from Germany.

Max length: 5¼ inches (13.5 cm)

Syrian hamster ★

The Syrian hamster was originally called the golden hamster because of its natural fur color. Now, many other colors exist, ranging from white and cream to brown and black. This hamster must be kept on its own to stop it from fighting with others. You are unlikely to see a Syrian hamster eating. Instead, it will fill its cheek pouches, then carry its food back to its nest.

Tt

Max length: 6 inches (15 cm)

Tarantula ★★

The tarantula is a pet to look at rather than handle. It has a painful bite and its hairs can cause a rash or even blindness if it flicks them into your eye. The tarantula's body is fragile, and if it is dropped it is likely to die. Female tarantulas have a long lifespan of up to 20 years, but males may only live for two years.

Fact
Some tarantulas live in trees, where they hunt young birds. Others are found in underground burrows, from where they ambush prey.

Max length: 2¾ inches (7 cm)

Tiger barb ★★

The stripy tiger barb is one of the most popular tropical fish. It is so-called because its color and markings look like the striped patterning of a tiger. Unfortunately, tiger barbs can be aggressive—they snap at the fins of other fish in their aquarium. When breeding, the female tiger barb can lay up to 700 eggs at a time.

Tokay gecko ★★

Max length: 12 inches (30 cm)

Being a larger lizard, the tokay gecko needs to live in a large enclosure with sturdy branches for climbing. This lizard is fascinating to watch, but should be handled with care because it can be aggressive. Its name comes from the sound that it makes: "to-kay! to-kay!" Tokay geckos eat insects, and some even eat mice.

Tortoiseshell cat ★

Average height: 9 inches (23 cm)

All tortoiseshell cats have some red and black areas in their coats, but their markings are very individual—no two look exactly the same. Some also have white patches and are known as tortoiseshell-and-white. Almost all tortoiseshell cats are female, and they make excellent, devoted mothers. Tortoiseshell coloration is seen in many other breeds today.

Uu

Max length: 2½ inches (6 cm)

Ulrey's tetra ★★

Many creatures are named after a person, and this is the case with Ulrey's tetra. It is named after a man called Albert Ulrey.

Ulrey's tetras need to be kept in a group, called a school, because they are friendly and will often swim together. Ulrey's tetras will also live happily alongside other fish, as long as they are not aggressive. These fish like to hide, so plants should be included in their aquarium.

Fact
The male umbrella cockatoo has black eyes, while the hen's are a dark reddish-brown. Their lifespan can be similar to that of humans.

Max length: 17 inches (43 cm)

Umbrella cockatoo ★★★

The long, white crest feathers of this cockatoo look like an umbrella covering its head. The cockatoo raises its crest feathers when it is excited or frightened, often screeching loudly at the same time. It is an intelligent and affectionate member of the parrot family, requiring a lot of care.

Vietnamese pot-bellied pig

Max length: 3 feet (91 cm)

★★★

The Vietnamese pot-bellied pig can become very tame; it can even be taught to walk with a harness and leash! Unfortunately, these intelligent pets have some habits that mean you may not want to keep them indoors. For example, they enjoy wallowing in muddy pools. The mud dries on their skin, which helps protect their bodies against sunburn and insect bites.

Volpino Italiano

Max height: 12 inches (30 cm)

★

The volpino Italiano makes an excellent guard-dog. Wary of strangers, it will not hesitate to bark at passers by. It adapts well to indoor life, but requires a lot of brushing. Most volpino Italianos have a pure white coat.

Ww

Max length: 1½ inches (4 cm)

White Cloud Mountain minnow ⭐

This beautiful fish is named after its homeland in the White Cloud Mountains in China. It is sometimes called Tan's fish in honor of the man who discovered it. It is not a true tropical fish because it comes from cool mountain streams—so it can be kept in an unheated aquarium in a warm room. Its bright coloration usually fades as it becomes older. Meteor minnows are a rare type of White Cloud Mountain minnow with long fins.

Fact
White's tree frog has anti-viral and anti-bacterial substances in its skin. One of these is used to regulate human blood pressure.

Max length: 4 inches (10 cm)

White's tree frog ⭐⭐

As its name suggests, White's tree frog clambers around on branches rather than living on the ground. Its enlarged, sticky toe pads even allow it to climb up glass. These frogs are often green, but some have areas of white on their bodies. They tend to look fat and flabby and have rubbery skin. They can live for as long as 15 years.

Wild Abyssinian cat ★

Average height: 9 inches
(23 cm)

This rare cat is not wild by nature, in spite of its name. It was originally bred from homeless domestic cats living on the streets of Singapore. The wild Abyssinian looks like the Abyssinian itself (see page 8), but it is bigger and has dark tabby spots on its body. It is known to be independent and friendly.

Max length: 2¾ inches (7 cm)

Wrestling halfbeak ★★

The wrestling halfbeak has a short upper jaw and a longer lower jaw that can easily be damaged. Males often lock their jaws together in a test of strength. They may remain locked like this for up to half an hour, until the weaker fish breaks away. These fish require more care than others, especially in the preparation of their living space.

Xx

Max length: 4½ inches (11 cm)

Xenopus frog ★★

The xenopus frog, also called the African clawed frog, has a flat body shape. Its natural color is gray, but there are also albino xenopus, which are creamy-white with pink eyes. It lives in shallow water and its strong hind legs allow it to swim fast. The xenopus frog's aquarium needs to be carefully prepared.

Max height: 11 inches (28 cm)

Xoloitzcuintli ★★

(Say it: Cho-lo-etz-queent-lee)

This intelligent breed is also known as the Mexican hairless dog. Its skin is dark and the only wisps of hair are found on its head and at the tip of its tail. Called the xolo dog for short, this breed is cheerful with family and shy with strangers.

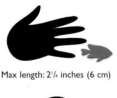

Max length: 2¼ inches (6 cm)

X-ray tetra ★★

Looking at this fish is like seeing an X-ray picture, because you can see its bones through its transparent body. This active fish is not aggressive toward other fish. It prefers shady surroundings, and the color of its fins will be brighter when the aquarium lights are dim.

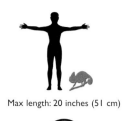

Max length: 20 inches (51 cm)

Yemeni chameleon ★★

Chameleons have long tongues with sticky tips—their tongues are one and a half times their body length! The Yemeni chameleon moves very slowly so as not to frighten its insect prey, then it fires its tongue out like a dart to grab them. It has very good eyesight and is able to swivel each eye individually. It can also change its color, depending on its mood, the light, and the temperature.

Fact
This chameleon is unusual: unlike any of its relatives, it eats plants regularly, possibly as a way of obtaining extra water.

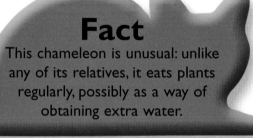

Max length: 4¼ inches (11 cm)

Zebra finch ★

The black-and-white striped feathers on the chest of the cock zebra finch help explain the bird's name. This exotic bird lives in large flocks in the wild. It is recommended that the zebra finch is kept as a pet with others of its kind. It requires feeding, cleaning, and toys in its cage.

Glossary

Amphibian An air-breathing, cold-blooded vertebrate. Most amphibians lay jelly-covered eggs.

Ancestors Older relatives of an animal, which may already be extinct.

Aquarium A glass or plastic container that is filled with water and is home to fish.

Aviary A large enclosure for birds made with panels of wire mesh. An outdoor aviary also has a shedlike shelter where the birds go when the weather is bad.

Barbels The projections seen around the mouths of fish such as catfish, which help them find food.

Bill The upper and lower jaws of a bird.

Billy A male goat.

Bird A vertebrate with feathers that breeds by laying eggs.

Breed A group of animals within a species with a similar appearance. Breeds are often developed by deliberate selection.

Breeding Producing young.

Breeding period The time when an animal is having young.

Buck A male rabbit.

Cat One of a group of furry, four-legged mammals. The cat family includes lions, tigers, and cheetahs.

Cichlid A type of fish that often looks after its young.

Cock A male bird.

Cold-blooded An animal whose body temperature depends on the temperature of its surroundings.

Glossary

Crest A raised area of fur, feathers, or skin, usually on an animal's head.

Diabetes An illness that is linked to sugar in the diet.

Doe A female rabbit.

Dog A mammal that is a member of a family that includes both foxes and wolves.

Domestic An animal with wild ancestors that has changed its behavior, having been kept and bred by people for many years.

Fish Cold-blooded creatures with fins and a backbone that live in water.

Gills The organs that allow tadpoles and fish to take oxygen from water, so they can breathe underwater. The gills are on each side of the head, behind the eyes.

Grooming Taking care of the skin or fur of an animal.

Harness A strap that attaches to the chest of an animal so it can be held on a leash.

Hen A female bird.

Insect An invertebrate with three pairs of legs, whose body is made up of three parts: the head, thorax, and abdomen.

Invertebrate An animal without a backbone.

Iodine A chemical that is needed in a tiny amount to allow tadpoles to change into adult amphibians.

Kid A young goat.

Glossary

Koi A large type of fish belonging to the carp family.

Leash A line for leading or restraining an animal.

Lizard A type of reptile with a scaly skin and a tail.

Longhair An animal with a long coat.

Lop A rabbit with ears that hang down at the sides of its head.

Maintenance The care given to ensure the well-being of an animal.

Mammal A warm-blooded animal that suckles milk from its mother.

Matted Hair that has become stuck together, sometimes because it has not been groomed.

Molt To lose hair or feathers in order for them to be replaced.

Newt A type of amphibian with a tail.

Omnivore An animal that eats both meat and plants.

Parrot A bird with a hook-shaped bill, which grips a perch with two toes in front and two behind.

Pellets Specially-made hard food, usually sold in packets.

Predator An animal that hunts other animals.

Prey An animal that is hunted by another animal.

Reptile A cold-blooded creature with scales. Females may have live babies or lay eggs.

Retriever A type of dog which was first bred to bring back birds that had been shot.

Rex A wiry type of coat, as in rex guinea pigs, or a very soft coat, as in the case of rex rabbits.

Glossary

Rodent A small mammal with two pairs of incisor teeth at the front of its mouth.

Shorthair An animal with a short coat.

Sled A vehicle that can be pulled over snowy ground by certain types of dogs.

Snake A reptile with a long body and no legs.

Spider An invertebrate with four pairs of legs.

Tabby A cat with particular dark markings on its coat. There are different types of tabby patterning, but all tabby cats have an M-shaped marking on their forehead.

Tadpole A young amphibian that lives in water and breathes through its gills, before changing into an adult.

Tame To make an animal's behavior more suitable for being a pet.

Tentacles The armlike projections of underwater invertebrates, used to grab food, feel, and sometimes sting.

Toe pads The swollen areas on the feet of tree frogs and some lizards that help them climb without slipping.

Tolling The way hunters attract ducks.

Vertebrate An animal with a backbone.

Vivarium A glass tank used to house reptiles or amphibians.

X-ray A special type of photograph that shows the position of bones inside the body.

Index

A
Abyssinian cat 8
American shorthair cat 8
Anemone fish 9
Angelfish 9
Angora rabbit 10
Axolotl 10

B
Bearded dragon 11
Bengal cat 11
Betta 11
Birman cat 12
Bombay cat 12
British shorthair cat 13
Budgerigar 13
Burmese cat 13

C
California spangled cat 14
Canary 14
Chihuahua 15
Chinchilla 15
Chipmunk 16
Cockatiel 16
Corn snake 17
Corydoras catfish 17

D
Damselfish 18
Degu 18
Devon rex 19
Discus 19
Dutch rabbit 19

E
Eskimo dog 20
Exotic cat 20

F
Ferret 21
Finnish spitz 21
Fire salamander 22
Four-eyed fish 22

G
Garter snake 23
German shepherd 23
Goat 23
Golden retriever 24
Goldfish 24
Gray parrot 25
Green iguana 25
Greyhound 25

H
Hatchetfish 26
Havanese dog 26
Hermit crab 27
Himalayan cat 27

I
Ibizan hound 28
Indian walking stick 28

J
Japanese bobtail cat 29
Japanese fire-bellied newt 29
Jewel cichlid 30
Jird 30

K
Keeshond 31
Kingsnake 31
Kissing gourami 31
Koi 32
Korat cat 32

L
Leopard gecko 33
Llama 33
Lop, dwarf rabbit 34
Lovebird 34

M
Maine coon cat 35
Manx cat 35
Molly 36
Mongolian gerbil 36
Mouse 37
Mynah bird 37

N
Neon tetra 38
Netherland dwarf rabbit 38
Norwegian forest cat 39
Nova Scotia duck tolling retriever 39

O
Old English sheepdog 40
Orange chromide 41
Orfe 41
Oscar 41

P
Painted turtle 42
Paradise fish 42
Parrotlet 43
Persian cat 43
Platy 44
Pygmy hedgehog 44

Q
Quail, button 45
Quetzal cichlid 45

R
Ragdoll cat 46
Rat 46
Rat snake 47
Rex rabbit 47
Russian hamster 48
Russian shorthair cat 48

S
Scottish fold cat 49
Siamese cat 49
Society finch 50
Sphynx cat 50
Swordtail 51
Syrian hamster 51

T
Tarantula 52
Tiger barb 52
Tokay gecko 53
Tortoiseshell cat 53

U
Ulrey's tetra 54
Umbrella cockatoo 54

V
Vietnamese pot-bellied pig 55
Volpino Italiano 55

W
White Cloud Mountain minnow 56
White's tree frog 56
Wild Abyssinian cat 57
Wrestling halfbeak 57

X
Xenopus frog 58
Xoloitzcuintli 58
X-ray tetra 58

Y
Yemeni chameleon 59

Z
Zebra finch 59